To Lily and Kiki S.L.

Text by Elena Pasquali
Illustrations copyright © 2010 Steve Lavis
This edition copyright © 2010 Lion Hudson

The moral rights of the author and illustrator
have been asserted

A Lion Children's Book
an imprint of
Lion Hudson plc
Wilkinson House, Jordan Hill Road,
Oxford OX2 8DR, England
www.lionhudson.com
Paperback ISBN 978 0 7459 6188 0
Hardback ISBN 978 0 7458 6253 5

First UK edition 2010
1 3 5 7 9 10 8 6 4 2 0
First US edition 2011
1 3 5 7 9 10 8 6 4 2 0

A catalogue record for this book is available
from the British Library

Typeset in 16/22 ITC Berkeley Oldstyle BT
Printed in China January 2011 (manufacturer LH06)

Distributed by:
UK: Marston Book Services Ltd, PO Box 269, Abingdon, Oxon OX14 4YN
USA: Trafalgar Square Publishing, 814 N Franklin Street, Chicago, IL 60610
USA Christian Market: Kregel Publications, PO Box 2607, Grand Rapids, MI 49501

Mrs Noah's Vegetable Ark

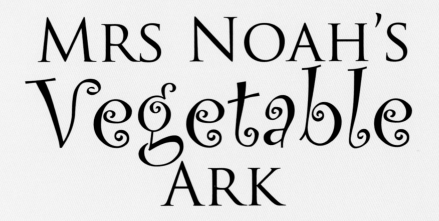

Elena Pasquali

Illustrated by Steve Lavis

LION
CHILDREN'S

Mrs Noah muttered as she watered her vegetable garden.

"It's so dry these days," she complained. "I've never known it so dry."

She looked up to where her husband was busy with his new project.

"What on earth does Noah think he's doing building an ark?" she asked aloud. "This place has never flooded.

"Although," she added, "we could use a bit of rain."

The rain didn't come and Mrs Noah's watering was worth the effort.

That summer, the beans ran up their poles and the carrots grew so long that they almost lifted themselves out of the ground.

The fruit on the trees grew plump and ripe, and on their trailing vine, the pumpkins were magnificent.

But how did those two rabbits get in and start nibbling the lettuces?

Mrs Noah opened the gate to shoo them out – and what a sight she saw.

"Oh, Noah!" she sighed. "I didn't think you'd go this far. Are you really going to load the animals onto your ridiculous rescue ark?"

Noah simply nodded: the nod of someone who is very, very sure that what they are doing is right, however foolish it may seem.

And Mrs Noah got to thinking.

If Noah really was right about a flood…

and if he really needed to save the animals…

THEN WHAT ABOUT HER VEGETABLE GARDEN?

She set to work.

She made little bags to put over the seed heads to collect the seeds.

She put the rhubarb into pots and the raspberry canes into pans.

She dug up the fruit trees and wrapped the roots in sacking, earth and all.

Then she got all the animals to load her vegetable garden onto the ark.

The very next day, the sky that had been clear blue for so long turned cloudy.

From the shelter of the ark, everyone watched as the puddles grew and then joined up.

Mrs Noah dabbed her eyes as she watched one forgotten tree float away, cradled in the old pumpkin vine.

"Perhaps it will be all right," she said. "Plants can be very determined to survive."

But then it was time for getting on with keeping her household together on the ark.
  Once the vegetables for stew were neatly chopped and simmering,
Mrs Noah had time to plant some seeds.

The rain was astonishing and a flood spread over the world. As the days turned into weeks, the seeds grew. They produced leaves and fruit and yet more seeds. Out on deck, the trees bore another harvest.

"What would have happened without all these lovely fresh vegetables and fruit?" Mrs Noah asked proudly. "We'd have had vitamin deficiencies, that's what."

Even when the rain stopped, the ark was left alone on a sea of water.
The plants grew and grew and grew.

  Mrs Noah's vegetable ark grew more magnificent, even as, unnoticed,
the flood ebbed away.

  Then…

Whoa! What was that?

One day the ark ran aground on a mountain top.

When everyone had picked themselves up and tidied the scattered vegetables,
Noah sent one of the doves to look for land.

It came back with a fresh green twig in its beak.

"That could be from my tree!" cried Mrs Noah in excitement.
"An olive was the one we forgot. After all, I did prune it for the
flood so that it would produce fine new shoots."

"Well, my dear," said Noah, "God only told me to take care
of the animals.

"But we can all be glad that you took care of the plants."

Soon the world was dry.

A rainbow spread from heaven to earth as
the animals dashed away to find new homes.

Mrs Noah was able to plant a new vegetable garden
as the whole world grew green and beautiful.